T0149705

THE KEY TO
Happiness

Tamar Salas

BALBOA.PRESS
A DIVISION OF HAY HOUSE

Balboa Press books may be ordered through booksellers or by contacting:

Balboa Press
A Division of Hay House
1663 Liberty Drive
Bloomington, IN 47403
www.balboapress.com.au
1 (877) 407-4847

Because of the dynamic nature of the Internet, any web addresses or
links contained in this book may have changed since publication and
may no longer be valid. The views expressed in this work are solely those
of the author and do not necessarily reflect the views of the publisher,
and the publisher hereby disclaims any responsibility for them.

The author of this book does not dispense medical advice or prescribe the use
of any technique as a form of treatment for physical, emotional, or medical
problems without the advice of a physician, either directly or indirectly. The
intent of the author is only to offer information of a general nature to help
you in your quest for emotional and spiritual well-being. In the event you use
any of the information in this book for yourself, which is your constitutional
right, the author and the publisher assume no responsibility for your actions.

Any people depicted in stock imagery provided by Getty Images are
models, and such images are being used for illustrative purposes only.
Certain stock imagery © Getty Images.

Print information available on the last page.

ISBN: 978-1-5043-2021-4 (sc)
ISBN: 978-1-5043-2022-1 (e)

Balboa Press rev. date: 01/08/2020

Dedication

I dedicate this small booklet to you,
dear reader, and to all the souls of
humanity who are searching for a way
home and seeking lasting happiness.
May the light of the universe shine
for all of us from within.

Contents

Contents

Acknowledgements

I would like to acknowledge all the people who have made this book possible, especially all my teachers of every school of thought I have chosen to learn from who, both directly and indirectly, have taught me so much. I also acknowledge the wisdom of Wing Chun kung fu, the wisdom of Kabbalah the science of the soul. In addition, I thank the masters in the field of integral NLP, my favourite teacher George Faddoul. Thank you all from the bottom of my heart for being part of my path and my journey towards discovering lasting happiness and lasting fulfilment.

I am also grateful to my friends and family who, by way of a cosmic connection, have made my journey of understanding, growth, appreciation, love, and observation possible.

Introduction

Dear Reader:

The reason why I decided to write *The Key to Happiness* is because daily, since I was a child, I have felt the pain of humanity.

While growing up, I always wondered why we as humans seem to be so eager to ascribe to a reason to suffering and a reason to pain—and not just a reason but also an opportunity, in that pain, chaos, and suffering are all an inevitable part of our lives.

In short, it seemed to me from a young age that the acceptance of the pain around me was far greater than the acceptance of living a life of abundance and lasting happiness.

I grew up in Santiago, Chile. My parents divorced when I was five years old. At five years old I got to be a spectator. When you are five, you are awake, and paradoxically you don't have much choice in decision-making because of your age, so you're in a position of just watching what's happening around you. In watching the people in my surroundings, I discovered that they all suffered a great deal because of what had happened between my mother and father. My father left my mother suddenly, without any prior notice.

Living through this scenario in my life, I felt as though my entire family had fought for years individually, trying to understand what had occurred, without deep reasoning, ultimately to find inner happiness. This seemed strange to me. I did feel that everything that had happened around the painful situation was "normal"—or at least we would say it was. We are human, and there is a process by which we filter emotional pain and deal with it. Sometimes this process takes longer than necessary, and sometimes it doesn't. Sometimes we're able to move on quickly and happily continue creating our future in the best way possible.

I did feel the loss of my estranged father after he left, also I was very fortunate to have had the immensely loving and nurturing support of my grandparents, my mother (who always took care of me), my aunts, and my entire family, by whom I felt protected and loved. In all of this I observed the pain of my family all around me, not only in the manner in which they dealt with how my father had left but also in the way they lived life in general. I guess living and viewing this situation allowed me to see and feel through the lens of a five year old the uncertainty and emotional pain also amongst the people outside my immediate family. In and out of school, for example, I felt the emotional struggle of other single moms, I saw the pain of their loss and discomfort, almost as if moving through life without closure.

So, I began to question what to this today appears to me to be a worldly phenomenon: the free acceptance of the experience of psychological pain, emotional pain, physical pain, and spiritual pain, covering the entirety of humankind across the globe, even almost before it happens. This questioning led me to think that just as we are creators of our own happiness, we are also the perpetrators and prolonging creators of our own pain and suffering.

Now, is this a conscious choice? Or is it an unconscious one, perhaps?

Within these short chapters, I present to you, dear reader, what has been obvious to me since childhood as some of the common presenting issues and frames of mind that prevent us from achieving internal lasting happiness and personal fulfilment.

Fifteen years ago, at the age of twenty-two, I faced one of the most difficult periods of my life. I felt forced to make the biggest and most powerful decision of my life: the decision to be happy.

All of us, at some point in our lives, must face the pain of losing dear loved ones, relationship break-ups, lost opportunities, downsized careers, job loss, and the like. These things seem to cloud the conscious decision-making process of gratitude. Being at peace oftentimes eludes us.

Daily we offer reasons and justifications for being upset. We willingly collect these experiences for as long as we consciously or unconsciously desire to do so.

I see in people's lives their need to be happy. And in trying to find happiness, they see happiness as a need rather than as a chance to embrace a new opportunity for lasting abundance and joy. I witness more and more, with questioning in my heart, the inability of society to find lasting happiness and paradoxically how close we are to attaining it each and every second of the day.

You may feel that this sounds pessimistic, but indeed it is the opposite. My only objective is to outline some of our presenting issues, those things which are rather obvious in our day-to-day but are hardly looked at through the lens of personal change and personal transformation.

In my heart, I know we know what happiness is, because when we are happy and content, we seldom question how we got that way. The important question is, why do we leave happiness unattended to until we find ourselves in trouble again? And how do we make happiness last?

As I sit here and write these paragraphs, I have an awareness that you will be reading this little booklet one day, and that day is today for you. It makes me happy to know that in having decided to read this, you want to put an end to your personal chaos and the suffering in your life by seeking to deeply understand what truly makes you happy. And that, my dear friend, makes me truly happy.

I feel that it is my duty to write this message for you, dear reader of this book.

In our lives, we seem to be looking for happiness in all the wrong places, from morning to night, and often we go to sleep at night without having found the answer to the question of what has caused our unhappiness. And when we wake up the next day, we deal with our problems in the very same way that we created them.

You and I know that in order to solve a problem, one must first look for what created said problem. The reason why most problems in our lives remain unsolved is because of our inability to get to the bottom of our own personal understanding of *how we think*. And even if we admit to ourselves and to the world how we think, we seldom want to believe that it is indeed our own way of thinking that is causing us grief, and we certainly don't think that we need to make any personal changes. We'd rather look at our next-door neighbours and feel envious, wondering how they have found their happiness. Seldom do we look deep enough inside ourselves to find and create our own happiness.

Oftentimes we even look for shortcuts or else neglect our issues by being busy with work, family, and so on, hoping that perhaps time will take care of our unresolved unhappiness. Or we may even go around blaming the world as the cause of our own unhappiness and personal dissatisfaction.

We seem to want to believe that the cause of our happiness is simply out there, somewhere where we haven't been before. It's almost as if we just completely give in to life on the outside and completely forget life on the inside, completely forgoing the infinite, abundant universe that each of us as human beings is fortunate to possess in each and every lifetime.

It is my wish that we as human beings on this earth begin to deeply search ourselves for our life's purpose; grow old and wise by learning to share unconditionally, learning to love ourselves, coming to understand love, and learning to nurture one another and walk side by side without prolonging our personal suffering.

How do we simply get to the bottom of our own pain and dare to transform it?

Chapter 1

There Are No Shortcuts to Happiness

If ever we choose a shortcut to create happiness,
we must know it will be the long way
around, with happiness never to be found.

There is a problem with wanting to take shortcuts to attain happiness, and the problem is that shortcuts prevent us from finding a long-term solution to our problems. Therefore, shortcuts prevent us from growing and from ever understanding our true potential.

Trying to find a shortcut to our happiness or success is in fact an effort to search for instant gratification, and we do that completely subconsciously all day long in our search for happiness. We seek short-lived experiences in order to receive short bursts of immediate happiness all day long, starting from an early morning coffee and moving on to reacting negatively to our problems during the day, finishing up in spiritual exhaustion at the end of the day.

Where is the genius behind this behaviour?

To find lasting happiness, we must restrict our need for instant gratification.

How do we do that? Do we look for happiness the long way around?

Not exactly. You see, the reason why we do most things in life isn't necessarily to find our place of ultimate purpose. Your ultimate personal purpose is completely different from my ultimate personal purpose, but we each must begin by wanting to discover what it is we are here to do, beyond what we may call mundane day-to-day actions, the actions of going to work to cover some of our expenses and provide for our family.

That is not our ultimate purpose.

When our lives become all about working to put a roof over our heads, we have lost our ultimate fulfilling purpose. Well, perhaps we have not lost it completely but have just misplaced it, wrapped it up in becoming busy with the shortcut process of trying to attain a certain level of happiness to achieve short-term results, living in survival mode.

Now do you see why shortcuts to happiness don't work?

I will challenge your beliefs in this small booklet so that we can arrive at happiness or at least at a beginning understanding of what your true purpose in life is, my friend.

Chapter 2

Why Being Busy Is Stealing Our Happiness

The positives and negatives of becoming busy with work, family, and friends are intertwined in our way of thinking.

How can we think beyond this paradigm, beyond this need to be so busy that we forget what's truly important to our spiritual evolution?

How can we shift our minds so we may then begin to unleash our soul's true potential?

If we have an issue, for example, and we want to get the best possible outcome for ourselves and our family, coworkers, or friends, we've first got to look at how we approach the issue at hand without becoming reactive or impulsive and as a consequence, sooner or later, becoming angry, sad, lost, confused, overwhelmed, and irritated— not because of any external elements but rather because of our default way of thinking.

The solution to our presenting issues has never been about changing the outside situations in any way, shape, or form to make things better. We have enough personal experience to say that if we have an issue with someone at work and we move to a different city only because of this one issue, the same scenario will likely occur again until we internally resolve the issue by means of engaging in introspection and finding where the root cause of the problem lies.

To give you a clearer example, today I coach clients how to live happier lives and how to embrace their true potential. I have a client who once asked me, "How did you turn your life around? I am so stuck that I don't know what to do to move from this place."

My answer to her was "I questioned my values and what I really wanted in life. I determined what I was prepared to give back, and I sought to expand my mind, body, and spirit."

She said, "But how?"

I answered, "I came to a point in my life where my only real choice was to admit to myself that I needed to change."

I then asked her, "What is your biggest pain point right now?"

She said, "Money and family."

"OK," I said, "so what would you like to do moving forward?"

She replied, "Get out of debt."

My reply was "OK, so let me guess. You want to free yourself from debt and spend more quality time with family, correct?"

"Yes," she answered immediately.

"So tell me what's stopping you from achieving all the things you want in life."

"Money."

"OK, how does a person make more money?" I asked.

She replied, "By getting a second job and working more."

"Tell me, how big is your debt, how long do you think it will take you to pay it off, and do you have a budget?" I asked.

She told me the size of the debt and said that it was almost impossible for her to pay it off because every time she had to make a payment, other expenses appeared. As a result, the debt kept growing bigger, especially with the accruing interest.

Well, here we clearly see that money wasn't the problem. My client was lacking financial literacy and a self-investing attitude. Money and change are by-products of who we are.

There's a famous quote by an unknown author: "If you were born poor, it's not your fault. Dying poor is."

The solution to all our problems that lead us to be unhappy has 100 per cent to do with our ability to cool off and seek to understand the bigger reason behind our problems.

That bigger reason is ourselves.

I would like to share with you one of the most proactive ways to resolve your personal issues. The Proactive Formula.

Pause first, take a deep breath in and out and then say the following:

OK, I have this problem right now with [so-and-so or such-and-such], and in my busy, rushed, cloudy, reactive state of mind, I cannot resolve it to achieve the best possible outcome for everyone. So the best thing that I can do is share my time with others with the intention to allow for clarity. Once my head is clear, I will find a solution to my problems, no matter what comes in front of me, and I will commit to setting aside a special time to dig deep and confront my own personal issues once and for all. Then I can be a better conduit of love, understanding, and happiness for everyone in my life. My state of lasting happiness depends on it.

The normal approach to problem-solving in our day-to-day lives is that we take the shortcut to a solution, which only brings about momentary, illusory happiness and much pain and suffering in the long term. But most of our problems can be avoided by simply deciding to pay closer attention to our own approach to happiness in the first place.

We've become accustomed to sweeping our problems under the carpet and deciding it is easier to forget about our own issues and focus on somebody else's problems.

At the same time, or on its own worth, we've become accustomed to receiving energy from instant gratification by way of external aids. Instant gratification only lasts momentarily and will never solve any of our real problems. So in this predicament, we go from being in a sad state to quickly shifting to a happy state and then quickly returning to the same emotional state we were in before.

A great example of how we begin at a young age to cultivate this method of achieving momentary pleasure is the first time our parents give us a taste of something pleasant when we are crying and nagging. The easiest solution is to give us something to shut us up.

Now where is the genius in us, repeating the same patterns over and over again throughout our lives without questioning them or arriving at real happiness?

It seems the quickest answer to happiness for all of us was at an early stage embedded in us, which led us ultimately to believe in short bursts of bliss. When did this clever idea begin for humanity, and why do we keep repeating this cycle?

Why are we allowing simple stresses of our day to day to rule in our lives? Why are we preventing ourselves from realizing the freedom of complete fulfilment?

Are we still holding on to the hope that time will heal everything?

Chapter 3

The "Time Will Heal" Frame of Mind

The "time will heal" frame of mind, for most of us, is what keeps us from achieving our true potential.

I'm not referring to the faith that one carries within in order to create miracles. I'm merely referring to the practical resolutions that one must make in order to understand happiness. Therefore, in this context, hope alone cannot solve any of our problems. If you don't believe me, please sit alone under the hot desert sun and read this book without any access to water. I hope that you don't become thirsty, because water will not turn up for you while you sit as a result of your hoping it will come to you.

The problem with hoping that time will take our problems away and that they will be banished as if by some merciful miracle of the gods is that hope, most of the time, must be accompanied by an action. Immediate, decisive action must be taken in order to get the energy of hope or miracles to work.

Hope arises when one is not able to control a situation, but often one turns to hope as a last resort.

Why use hope as a last resort? Why not use it immediately?

Rather than letting time pass in the hope that it will heal everything, use hope and desire immediately with the frame of mind of *I must let go of this issue now so that I can have clarity to work on the problem in this moment and have the presence of mind not to get distracted from achieving ultimate peace of mind.* Have this desire present in your mind to such a degree that you know that for the sake of happiness, it will present you with the clarity you need to go above and beyond momentary bursts of happiness and ultimately travel beyond pain and suffering. It is when in the moment of pain we ask what is this trying to teach me rather than try to forget the pain and move on that miracles begin to work for us, we by proactively choosing to learn in the moment open up for ourselves the opportunities to achieve lasting fulfilment.

Each day as I experience first-hand the sadness and somehow connect with the suffering and uncertainty in our society, not just in those I meet in the course of my professional work and research but also in my personal life, I'm compelled to ask, when did we become so caught up in vouching for and believing in our own suffering? It is almost as if we sell ourselves on our own misery each day, without seeking for the key to the solution.

We employ many keys in our western part of the world with the illusion that the many time-consuming "solutions", such as instant coffee, luxury cars, brand-name products, alcohol, drugs, sex, food, becoming reactive, abusing our own given energy, screaming, ranting, shouting, breaking things, and smashing things, will relieve us from our internal pain. We throw it all out there in the name of *I wanna get happy now!*

Chapter 4

The "Not Now—I'm Going through Something" Way of Thinking

Have you ever noticed that we seem to go through a lot of things as humans?

Does it ever feel to you that we get stuck in going through things and that we almost excuse ourselves from receiving lasting happiness because we are going through something?

We've become almost addicted to our feelings of loss and despair, frankly and not so frankly reasoning with our fear, anxiety, and past experiences, dealing with anger and stress, and being somewhat proud of our ability to withstand stress and worry, not to mention our jealousy and personal dissatisfaction with life.

For each of us, our own suffering is real because we are living within the confines of our made-up minds created by our personal history, the sum total of all our significant emotional events, our self-influenced and self-created thought patterns, and in some cultures the addition of past lives attached to our reasoning and the beginning and ending of our karmic cycles.

Suffering in the human realm of life is real to me and to you reading this book; no one can take away how you or I feel about a certain event.

However, you and I alone have the power to stay in a situation, and by the same token we have the power to create a new experience of thriving personal growth and lasting fulfilment instantaneously if we so choose.

Why do some of us choose one or the other at any given time when there is an abundance of choice to acclimate our way of thinking to achieve lasting happiness?

Nonetheless, I expect and respect that each one of us has different lessons laid out for us to learn and, because of this, different experiences to live, to feel, and to overcome.

The guided path, though, to achieving lasting happiness lies in becoming a conscious creator of happiness—hence the reason why I feel in the depths of my core the desire to write this booklet and expose the key to happiness once and for all.

It is my wish that as you read this book, despair and the sense of being overwhelmed will be lifted from your life so, as a result, the world can shine brighter because you are now fully in it.

Chapter 5

The Key to Happiness

The key to happiness is to love yourself. That is the key.

The key to happiness is to love yourself. If you are not friends with yourself, you will find it very hard to make friends with and offer unconditional love to other people.

Without self love, it's very hard to love the situations that you're being placed in. It's very hard to enter a room where there is chaos and actually be OK with it.

The key to happiness is to continuously learn to love yourself through every stage of life.

That's the key to happiness. There is no other key.

With an abundance of self-love and self-happiness comes the abundance of everything else you need to deal with whatever it is you are working on in your life.

The key to happiness is self-love.

Love yourself each and every day.

This can be achieved by looking in the mirror, no matter how uncomfortable you feel.

To be at a place you've never been, you must do things you've never done.

Take a look in the mirror and tell yourself how much you love yourself.

Love and admire your hair, love your skin, love your body as the vehicle that accompanies you through life, love your soul, and so on as we begin to learn to love ourselves, our own light will shine brighter.

There are many reasons for why we get unhappy. Today in our modern society, we have a name for this; it is called a "First World problem".

We are unhappy about the way we look, or the kilos we've put on or the kilos we've lost. Our parents, our friends, our spouses, and we ourselves make us unhappy.

We become unhappy about little things, or for instance we get angry about what other people are putting in our food and contaminating it, and so on and so forth, we get angry without looking for the long-term solution to our unhappiness. These are external things that can only be removed from our personal sphere, and can only be completely removed from our illusory paradigm of what makes us happy, if we internally love ourselves. It's the only way.

If you love yourself today, you'll have fewer headaches tomorrow. It's the only way.

So, loving ourselves is the key to happiness.

There's no other key. There's no other reason for why we exist on this planet. We are here to learn to love ourselves, because for whatever part of our nature with which we've come into this world that isn't bringing us joy, we need to become aware of it and do our work to change it. If there's something that we don't like about ourselves that we think we can improve on, that's the key to happiness, self-recognition, and self-love. There's no other way to happiness.

If you love yourself today, you'll be able to pass on that love to other people, and that love will get passed on and passed on and passed on, unconditionally.

You know those moments when somebody shares their frustrations with you and the interaction is a little bit negative and you feel drained afterwards? That's because you are left affected by the negativity—with no judgement, of course. It's just what happens. So when we are angry and we share our frustrations and anger with somebody else, we are spreading that negativity, our own negativity. How can any of us be happy if we don't really understand the inside of our frustration and the inside of our own negativity?

Our own energy is what we need to harness and seek to understand.

I hope this is making sense.

Because the more positive we are with ourselves and with the world, the more happiness we are sharing and vibrationally emanating. And we pass it on and pass it on and pass it on.

And this is truly how we change the world.

When we see something negative on television, of course we are immediately affected, and that in itself changes our DNA. It changes our make-up because we are being affected by it. Consider the premise that everything we absorb can be regarded as an event in our lives. So what happens is that the day after a negative experience, we wake up angry because we didn't resolve that thing or event that affected us the day or night before.

So, in essence, every occurrence that happens in our lives that affects us in a negative way is something we need to resolve almost immediately by means of pausing, restricting, suspending, and resisting our need to react to external situations and by means of observing our inner self by using the proactive formula in Chapter 2.

What we need to resolve is our need to impulsively and nervously react to life. We must feel the need to remember whatever is happening around us, behind us, or in front of us—whatever is coming into our sphere—and if we don't resolve it when it happens, we carry it as a frustration on the inside. Later that frustration turns into negativity, which we pass on to other people. And not only that, but also it may manifest in other areas of our lives, because negativity needs to escape from our system if it doesn't escape by means of personal resolution it grows as a negative emotion. Therefore, by not choosing to become proactive, we are continuously creating unhappiness for ourselves and becoming easily frustrated. This leads us to be the type of human being who has bursts, little moments of happiness, and then becomes frustrated, and then has little moments of happiness, and then is being affected by what is going on outside continuously, never allowing the light of true fulfilment to enter into our lives.

So, the key to happiness is, truly and deeply love yourself.

Seek to deeply understand yourself. Discover what makes you angry and what makes you frustrated, discover what triggers you and how to change it so you can grow into the best version of you. Determine how you can change yourself in order to share more positive energy with the world so that you may then change the world by changing yourself. If you understand that all of us as a collective, starting with each of us individually, have all the power that it takes to change the world, then life then becomes fulfilling. And it becomes fulfilling because of the conscious, awakened responsibility to maintain a high level of happiness throughout the twenty-four hours of the day, the seven days of the week, the thirty (or twenty-eight or thirty-one) days of the month, and the three hundred sixty-five days of the year that is necessary if we are to spiritually contribute to ending the pain and suffering in our world. I want you to take this as an opportunity while you are reading this book and if you've read this far, I'm guessing it has made sense to you.

Happiness does not come from wanting little or from settling for second best. It does not come once we decide to give up on our dreams as a result of circumstances.

Happiness comes from the valuable work that we do to help keep the balance of good in the world tipped in our favour as a collective, acknowledging ourselves as the global living soul on our planet. This is the key to lasting happiness, working on ourselves daily so we may share our greatest, unlimited, best version of ourselves and spread personal, internal balance, healing, and joy.

The key to happiness entails a proactive way of looking towards the world afresh with a new set of inner eyes as we learn to love our journey and come to deeply love ourselves.

This, my friend, is the key to happiness. It is with all my heart that I share this message with you so that we as a collective, as a global soul, can help heal pain and suffering in our world and eradicate it from the realm of humankind.

Be well, and be true to yourself.

Light and blessings!

—Tamar Salas

About the Author

Tamar Salas

Tamar Salas is an entrepreneur, martial arts expert, lifestyle coach, and life strategist. She earned a sport coaching certification, specializing in martial arts instruction, and is skilled at Wing

Chun Kung Fu. She's also a certified master i-NLP practitioner and has practiced the spiritual wisdom of Kabbalah for more than eight years. Salas founded The Tamar Salas Research Centre of Autonomy in 2018 after 10 years of research. She's been reunited with her Father since the age of 12, adores her two cats and lives in Sydney where she teaches her holistic system of healing full time.

Printed in the United States
By Bookmasters